Supernatural Discipleship

Growing in the Torah Way

By

Kenneth S. Albin

Table of Contents

Introduction:
My Journey

My discipleship journey started over forty years ago! I know that seems like a long time, but I can remember like yesterday giving my life to the Lord at fifteen years of age at the kitchen table with my dad and stepmom. I grew up Jewish, was Bar Mitzvah'd, and went to four years of Hebrew school, but I knew nothing to say about my identity and heritage. After accepting the Jewish Messiah, a slow journey began that brought me right back to my roots. I thought being a believer in Yeshua was somehow separate and a "new" thing that was not connected anymore to the Old Testament Laws, Rituals, and Holidays. Of course, the stories were timeless, and the principles were still applicable, but other than that I was a New Testament man. As time went on, my life began to be wrecked when my wife forced this Jewish boy to visit Israel for the first time. As the plane landed, they were playing a video of men dancing and praising the Lord in jubilant songs. When I saw these Jewish men dancing, something in me broke and the tears would not stop! I was not looking to be wrecked, but it came suddenly and unexpectedly. I heard an inner voice saying, "Kenny, this is who you are, and you can't deny it any longer. I will use you to reach My People!". Since that day I have been back to the Holy Land many times and so began the journey of reconnecting myself and those whom I "teach" to the freedom and blessings of keeping the Torah and believing in Yeshua-Jesus as Messiah.

I used to tell people I was never discipled, but that is not true at all. I was discipled in an amazing way because my father-in-law trained me to follow him around and do what he was doing and see what he was seeing. When the Lord walked the earth, how were His disciples trained? They went everywhere with Him, seeing what He saw and doing what He did. Now my father-in-law loved the Word of God and was adamant about believing it and doing what it said. He did not know about the Torah Way of keeping God's days and ways, but what He did know, he believed in walking it out: things like holiness, obedience, faithfulness, giving, loving, serving, and studying. I thank God for my heritage. It is a good foundation and place to start. If you are reading this, don't despise your past and what you learned. Use that foundation and build your life with the zeal and knowledge of those who went before you and honor that heritage.

As a leader for over thirty years in ministry, I have struggled and talked with many about discipleship and how it seems that most of God's people have never been discipled. It is not because the pastors and leaders don't try. They do, just like I did. The problem is with the methodology and the premise of discipleship that we did not know about. We tried to disciple using a "worldly" or "soul-based" model that can't work because it is not rooted in nor aligned with God's Supernatural Discipleship Way. Have you ever heard anyone say something like, "We need to get back to the Book of Acts?". You might have even said that, and I believe it is a good place to start because it is there that we see a movement of discipleship and supernatural spiritual and physical growth. We will be digging deep into that in this book, and the teachings of Yeshua and Moses and how they taught and made disciples. What if I told you that scripture teaches that Abraham, the father of faith, made disciples too? Let's dive in and learn about this Supernatural Discipleship which is for you, now, and for those you lead so that together we can expand God's kingdom as we await Messiah's return to rule and reign.

Chapter One: Abraham made disciples

I love studying and doing the Torah portions. However, when I was first introduced to them, I fought hard to stay far away from what would be "just another thing" for fear of being accused of "trying to make everyone Jewish!" During the pandemic, in the summer of 2020, I was having Zoom meetings on Wednesdays, and I was teaching whatever was on my heart. One day someone from my congregation asked if I would teach them the Torah portions like I was learning. I tried to send this member to a good friend who was teaching them, but God convicted and reproved me for sending my sheep to someone else to learn Torah. I decided to teach the Torah portion on Zoom but not tell anyone what it was. After two weeks, the secret was out, and everyone loved it! What I didn't know or understand, at the time, was that it was part of the "Secret Sauce" in not only discipleship but also a life filled with blessings. Let's look at Abram before he became Abraham, and what he did.

Genesis 14:14 AMP **14** When Abram heard that his nephew [Lot] had been captured, he H7324 armed and led out his H2593_trained men, born in his own house, [numbering] three hundred and eighteen, and went in pursuit as far [north] as Dan.

When Lot was captured in the War of Kings, Abram launched a rescue mission with an army of 318 trained men. The English translation of "trained" men, at the root level, in Hebrew, is pointing us to "discipleship training". These men had been born, raised, and trained in Abram's house.

H2593 חָנִיךְ **chânîyk,** kaw-neek'; from H2596; initiated; i.e. practiced:— trained.

Root Word: H2596 חָנַךְ **chânak,** khaw-nak'; a primitive root; (compare H2614) properly, to narrow; figuratively, to initiate or discipline:— dedicate, train up.

Proverbs 22:6 Train up H2596 a child in the way he should go: and when he is old, he will not depart from it.

We don't know all the details, but Abram and Sarai were making disciples that had become like them. It is amazing to know that Father Abraham was a discipleship maker and these disciples defeated at least four kings' armies with all the kingdom's resources. These disciples were, what I like to say, "NO JOKE serious disciples", who had power and skill because they caught what was taught by their spiritual father Abram. The disciples of Abram were armed and filled up with what He had been teaching them. The word for armed or led out, in Hebrew, means to pour or empty out. It was Abram who had filled his disciples with the truth of Torah and now he was "emptying out" that Word of truth on those who had stolen his family member, Lot.

H7324 רוק **rûwq,** rook; a primitive root; to pour out (literally or figuratively), i.e. empty:—× arm, cast out, draw (out), (make) empty, pour forth (out).

There is much more in the scriptures to substantiate Abram's discipleship program.

Genesis 12:5 BST And Abram took Sara his wife, and Lot the son of his brother, and all their possessions, as many as they had got, and every soul which they had got in Charrhan, and they went forth to go into the land of Chanaan.

The Hebrew language is far more specific than the English translations, for it says that Abram and Sarai "made souls in the land of Haran". How do you make souls? You train them in the only tried and true discipleship model of apprenticeship. Even the Levites had a five-year apprenticeship program before they could do their calling to serve in the Holy Place. From the age of twenty-five until thirty years old the Levites were being trained to see and do as their teacher and older, more seasoned, leaders would teach, demonstrate, and model. Now Abraham, in Haran, is training a new generation to worship the God that revealed Himself to him at seventy-five years old. Abraham began to teach about the Living God and the Torah as was revealed personally to him. You could say Abraham had a testimony and was living the proof of the concept. You might be thinking, "Hey, they didn't have the Torah back then. It was not given until Israel left Egypt and arrived at Sinai". Well, not exactly. Look at what God says about Abraham.

Genesis 26:3-5 TLV3 Live as an outsider in this land and I will be with you and bless you—for to you and to your seed I give all these lands—and I will confirm my pledge that I swore to Abraham your father. 4 I will multiply your seed like the stars of the sky and I will give your seed all these lands. And in your seed all the nations of the earth will continually be blessed, 5 because Abraham listened to My voice and kept My charge, My mitzvot, My decrees, and My H8451(Torah) instructions."

H8451תּוֹרָה tôwrâh, to-raw'; or תֹּרָה tôrâh; from H3384; a precept or statute, especially the Decalogue or Pentateuch:—law.

The seed of the spiritual Torah was from before creation. Now Abraham was duplicating himself and multiplying his spiritual offspring by modeling the kindness, generosity, and selfless serving that he had learned. He was obeying the Torah, modeling it, and passing it down to his disciples, making spiritual deposits into his trained servants. He was teaching what he had learned, and it is believed that Abraham had a discipleship school that he was known for. People who wanted to learn about his God, the one true God, and not follow the prevalent idolatry, had to cross over to where Abraham lived. The people who came would become "Spiritual Hebrews" who followed the "Torah Way" taught to them by Abraham the Father of faith. Those who crossed over would leave idolatry and pagan ways to leave and cleave to Abraham's God known as El Shaddai.

We know according to the book of Romans that the Torah is spiritual. (Rom 7:22) It was the "spiritual" Torah Way that Abraham was using to train his disciples. Can you see the supernatural and exponential power and results it produced? Abraham had his small group of disciples, just 318, and they were so powerful that they subdued five kingdoms, brought back Lot, and all that was taken from the other four kingdoms. It is no wonder why we see Abraham giving the first and best of all the "tithe" to a representative of God's greater Kingdom named Melchizedek.

If we are to go back to the Book of Acts, then we must go back even further to the real roots of faith and training for reigning. That is where we will start our journey into supernatural discipleship. We have gone back to learn from our Father Abraham. I want to leave you in this chapter with an important verse that I believe many have disregarded or not recognized its value.

Jeremiah 6:16 CJB16 Here is what Adonai says: "Stand at the crossroads

and look;
ask about the ancient paths, 'Which one is the good way?' Take it, and you will find rest for your souls. But they said, 'We will not take it.'

If you are reading this book, you are being reminded of the ancient path and the good way that is timeless and will work in every place and generation. Many are at this crossroad, a place where you must choose which way to walk. For generations, the hidden mysteries and secrets of this Living Way have been covered up because of misunderstandings and confusion leading many people to reject the Torah, seeing it as bondage that Yeshua-Jesus came to free us from. This could not be further from the truth and we will be looking at this in detail later in the book. For now, open your sanctified imagination to the real and true revelation that is inherent in the true foundation and ancient path. This is how Abraham and Yeshua walked. Are we to be any different?

Proverbs 22:28 Remove not the ancient landmark, which thy fathers have set.

The ancient landmark and paths of the Father, unfortunately, have been removed since before the time of Constantine. A different path was forged and greatly promoted that mixed the Holy and the Profane. What is normal and called good today is very far from the foundations of faith that were taught by the Patriarchs,

Prophets, and those in the time of Yeshua and beyond to the book of Acts. What the new generation of ministry leaders has been taught and is teaching has not produced desirable results. Instead of making biblical disciples grounded in God's Torah, the new methods are producing shallow, self-centered, culture-driven, powerless, and weak believers. Discipleship must be driven by spirit and truth, not by the soul, natural wisdom, or common sense. Without the ancient paths and the Torah as a firm foundation, true discipleship will not occur. Do you remember the parable of the sower? There is only one out of four types of soil or ground that produces a harvest that will last and multiply. The ground is the good heart and that heart is described as the one who receives the seed of the Word and does not let it go! As we get back to growing the Torah way, we will discover that it is easy and light; a yoke you will want to put on because it is joining you to Yeshua.

Luke 8:15 AMP But as for that seed in the good soil, these are the ones who have heard the word with a good and noble heart, and hold on to it tightly, and bear fruit with patience.

Chapter Two:
Yeshua's Master Class

When we read the New Testament or, in Hebrew the "Brit Hadashah", we must remember not to think of it as completely new, but rather as a renewal and revelation of the covenant that was begun by our Father. Yes, He is your Father too, if you believe in Yeshua-Jesus. You get the Covenant and you get to walk in the rights, privileges, and responsibilities of that covenant relationship. Remember, the Bible is adamant about not changing what was written by adding or taking away from that word. This means if Yeshua was and is the Messiah, He would not be adding or changing what was written. Yeshua did not change the dietary laws nor did he teach or model sabbath breaking. When you study things like this in context, you will see that His teaching was perfectly in line with what the rabbinical scholars believed; that Messiah would clarify the Torah and teach the spirit as well as the letter of the word as can be seen in these Old and New Testament scriptures:

Deuteronomy 13:1 CJB Everything I am commanding you, you are to take care to do. Do not add to it or subtract from it.

Revelation 22:19 CJB 19 And if anyone takes anything away from the words in the book of this prophecy, God will take away his share in the Tree of Life and the holy city, as described in this book.

Both Testaments are very clear about changing or adding or taking away something that was given as scripture by and through the Holy Spirit. Moses himself received the Torah, mouth to mouth, and to think that somehow Yeshua-Jesus would annul it or change it because He was the Messiah might be on the verge of ludicrous. God is not fickle and according to the Word, He does not change. Many people have been taught a dispensational theology that is not rooted in scripture. If Yeshua did not change the Word, then why do so many people think He did? We have to deal with these "sacred cows" because they become stumbling blocks or hindrances to the supernatural, discipleship of the Torah way.

Matthew 5:17-20 CJB 17 "Don't think that I have come to abolish the Torah or the Prophets. I have come not to abolish but to complete. 18 Yes indeed! I tell you that until heaven and earth pass away, not so much as a yud or a stroke will pass from the Torah — not until everything that must happen has happened. 19 So whoever disobeys the least of these mitzvot and teaches others to do so will be called the least in the Kingdom of Heaven. But whoever obeys them and so teaches will be called great in the Kingdom of Heaven.

The very strong teaching of our

Lord is if you disobey the least commandment and teach that falsehood to others, then you will be the least in the kingdom. If you obey and teach others the least, then you will be the greatest in the Kingdom. Perhaps Yeshua did not understand His mission to destroy and make the law invalid like many teach today. Why didn't he tell the people something like, "Hey, you know Moses and the Pharisees teach you all this law stuff, but I am going to die, be buried, then raised on the third day so that none of that will matter anymore. Just believe and trust my work and all will be good. Forget that Torah stuff, it is just bondage!" Don't laugh! This is what most people believe today about the gospel and what Jesus came to do. But that is not what He said is it?

He said the greatest in the Kingdom will teach to do even the "least" of the commands. Now don't get me wrong, He would also teach that it was not just doing these physical commands, but doing them with a pure and good heart. He never taught the commands as a way to be saved, but to do them with a heart of love and service as a testimony of your belief and trust in the God of your salvation.

Matthew 23:23 TLV 23 "Woe to you, Torah scholars and Pharisees, hypocrites! You tithe mint and dill and cumin, yet you have neglected the weightier matters of Torah—justice and mercy and faithfulness. It is necessary to do these things without neglecting the others.

The Torah being spiritual was always to be lived by people who would allow their hearts to be transformed. Yes, Adonai told Israel that the Word should be in their heart. To live by the heart meant that the appetites, emotions, desires, and intellect of man's soul or "nephesh" would have to continually walk day by day and year by year honoring the Moedim, God's appointed times. They must also guard and do the weekly Shabbats, go three times a year to give first fruits, give honor and take care of the widow, strangers, orphans, and the poor. The only way to learn the Moedim is to do them. The only way to have faith is to live faith. The only way to mercy is through a demonstration. Actions of the hand follow the heart as well as the words of the mouth. The "Hebrew

Mindset" is somewhat different from the "Greek Mindset" which is about knowledge for the sake of knowledge. Since we are spiritual Hebrews, we must understand that knowledge is not true knowledge until it is lived and walked in. Head knowledge is different from heart knowledge rooted in the "doing" and "actions" of faith. This understanding is reiterated in the book of James.

James 1:22-25 TLV 22 But be doers of the word, and not hearers only, deluding yourselves. 23 For if anyone is a hearer of the word and not a doer, he is like a man who looks at his natural face in a mirror— 24 for once he looks at himself and goes away, he immediately forgets what sort of person he was. 25 But the one who looks intently into the perfect Torah, the Torah that gives freedom, and continues in it, not becoming a hearer who forgets but a doer who acts—he shall be blessed in what he does.

Since our book is about supernatural discipleship as our goal, then how does it come about? How can we get the supernatural results that Abraham and Yeshua saw? It starts with a heart that is willing to hear, to do, and to obey. The disciples of Yeshua got a three-year crash course from Rabbi Yeshua and we know it produced supernatural results because when Peter got up to speak on Shavuot-Pentecost, all the "acts" in the book of "Acts" turned the world upside down. The Supernatural Discipleship model is rooted in doing Torah, but most people don't even know what that looks like or means. We see today an awakening happening and it is wonderful. When God awakens you to this walk of obedience and the life that flows from it, you won't ever want to go back to living or being a disciple without this supernaturally charged and blessed life. Why? It works. The Torah Way works for you. I like to say it does the heavy lifting so I don't have to. This Torah Way does not need man's catch slogans, the latest themes, or movie titles to attract the people and keep their short-lived attention. The Torah Way to supernatural discipleship will be the very opposite and not satisfy your soul like Esau who craved that red stuff and sold his birthright for a pot of stew. Your spiritual birthright is this walk and way of the Messiah. This is the way you were meant to live, to thrive, to grow, and to go be a light to the nations and to make natural Israel jealous.

Before we look more at the book of Acts, let's stay in the gospels and see what Yeshua taught His disciples.

Matthew 28:18- 20 TLV   18 And Yeshua came up to them and spoke to them, saying, "All authority in heaven and on earth has been given to Me. 19 Go therefore and make disciples of all nations, immersing them in the name of the Father and the Son and the Ruach ha-Kodesh, 20 teaching them to observe all I have commanded you. And remember! I am with you always, even to the end of the age."

For years I thought like so many that teaching what Yeshua commanded was something different and brand new, like "love your neighbor as yourself" and that kind of thing. I never thought He was telling his disciples to train the people in Torah. Yet, that is exactly what He was saying: "Teach them to obey all I command you". That is strong language. Teach disciples obedience to all! I never saw that until very recently because my mind had been pre-programmed to think about only "grace" or "mercy". I never put together the fact that the "Living Eternal Word" wanted everyone to keep obeying the same Torah He had lived by, in complete faith and trust during His years on the earth. We know Yeshua never sinned and could not be Messiah if he walked contrary or indifferent to the Torah of Moses. In fact, Moses prophesied multiple times about one who would come and be like Him. Those who would follow Him would either be obedient or be destroyed. This is also the blessing of Judah, the line of Messiah.

Genesis 49:10 TLV10 The scepter will not pass from Judah nor the ruler's staff from between his feet, until he to whom it belongs will come. To him will be the **obedience** of the peoples.

Now we know the fullness of this has not come about but the prophecy is that one day all the peoples will obey. Yeshua told his disciples to have the people obey because it is necessary, not for salvation, but to live as a light and testimony of that salvation. The Torah is not contrary to grace and mercy; it is the way to live and walk in the blessings with supernatural power that cannot be explained or denied.

Look at this scripture on how Yeshua dealt with self-righteousness.

Luke 18:17-23 TLV   17 Amen, I tell you, whoever does not receive the kingdom of God like a little child will never enter it." 18 And a religious leader inquired of Yeshua, saying, "Good Teacher, what shall I do to inherit eternal life?" 19 "Why are you calling Me good?" Yeshua said to him. "No one is good except One—that is God. 20 You know the commandments: 'Do not commit adultery, do not murder, do not steal, do not give false testimony, honor your father and mother.'" 21 The man said, "All these I have kept since my youth." 22 When Yeshua heard this, He said to him, "One thing you still lack. Sell all, as much as you have, and distribute to the poor, and you will have treasure in heaven. Then come, follow Me." 23 But upon hearing these things, he became deeply distressed, for he was very rich.

A very rich man asked Yeshua a question about Eternal Life. This man was a leader and knew the answer, but how did Yeshua answer him? "You know the commandments". Why did Yeshua say the way to eternal life was through the commandments? Didn't our Lord know about the plan to do away with all the commandments? Why is he telling this man "You know the commandments"? Because the man "knew" them, but didn't. He was not willing to depart with the riches he had accumulated. He was not willing to unload those riches to receive greater riches and leave all to follow Messiah.

The Lord was showing this man, through the commandments, that his faith was not in God, but in his possessions. The Torah way means you have to become a child to receive the kingdom and that means you can't hold on tightly to selfish ways and trusting in wealth or riches. Your hands are to be holding tightly the commandments and the faith and resurrection of Yeshua. (Revelation 14:12)

Psalm 19:8-12 TLV Nothing is hidden from its heat. 8 The Torah of Adonai is

perfect,
 restoring the soul. The testimony of Adonai is trustworthy, making the simple wise. 9 The precepts of Adonai are right, giving joy to the heart. The mitzvot of Adonai are pure,
 giving light to the eyes. 10 The fear of Adonai is clean enduring forever. The judgments of Adonai are true and altogether righteous. 11   They are more desirable than gold, yes, more than much pure gold! They are sweeter than honey and drippings of the honeycomb. 12   Moreover by them Your servant is warned. In keeping them there is great reward.

The discipleship model of Yeshua is to keep and obey all the commandments. I never knew or put that together. In fact, as a local "pastor", I tried to make disciples my whole life. I have been a part of so many discipleship models, programs, teachings, and training with such good intentions. I have heard some great leaders and pastors say the same thing, "We aren't making disciples of the adults, the youth, nor the children, and the "church", statistically, is in big trouble". This probably is not news to you, especially if you live in America right now. You can't help but notice the attack of the enemy on moral standards, righteousness, or holiness, attempting to subvert all religious values to be "woke" to what is becoming the way and law of the land. How pertinent is the Torah now? I believe we need this Torah Way more than ever and we can, through God's help and by His Spirit, see a return and revival in our Land and the nations of the World, and yes, in Israel!

It's not by might, nor by power, but by my spirit, saith the LORD of hosts. (Zechariah 4:6 B)

Yeshua was and still is a Master discipleship maker. How did he do it? For what is believed to be three and a half years, the very young men that He called followed him, watched him work, worked with him, and finally were sent to do what they had seen him do. The book of Acts says: "These have been with Him". I love the expression "more is caught than taught". Now I am rethinking that. Although we must catch the spirit of our teacher, we must also catch his teaching and "doing". It is not one or the other, but both. When our

Lord called the disciples, they forsook all to follow him. Somehow we have forgotten that truth. It's not even talked about, forsaking all and leaving all for the Lord and the gospel. In the past, I did work in Russia and was told by many of the pastors that to come to faith in Russia you have to forsake all. You probably will lose your status, career, family, and friends and your new family is God's family. A high price but the people in Russia do it knowing the reward of obedience is greater than anything they give up.

Luke 14:33 "So likewise, whoever of you does not forsake all that he has **cannot be My disciple.**

Mark 3:14 **14** And he ordained twelve, that they should be with him, and that he might send them forth to preach,

When Yeshua called to himself the appointed twelve, they left all to be with him. This is still the call to discipleship; the price and the cost that is seldom mentioned. The culture today has dictated a different gospel; one that is "me" centered instead of Messiah centered. The twelve called to follow the Lord were willing to leave and cleave to the Lord to learn at His feet like Mary. They were willing to do this knowing one day they too would have disciples of their own. The Master Class given by our Lord had to be like no other school or apprentice program. Imagine the insight, depth, and revelation that was poured out like water into the thirsty souls of those first disciples. Remember they did not have the New Testament. So, what was the Lord teaching those disciples? What scriptures were they learning? Even in the time of the Book of Acts, the letters and apostolic writings were just being written. They were not published quite yet.

2 Timothy 3:14-17 TLV **14** You, however, continue in what you have learned and what you have become convinced of. For you know from whom you have learned, **15** and that from childhood you have known the sacred writings that are able to make you wise, leading to salvation through trusting in Messiah Yeshua. **16** All Scripture is inspired by God and useful for teaching, for reproof, for restoration, and for training in righteousness, **17** so that the person belonging to God may be capable, fully

equipped for every good deed.

I believe a seat at the Lord's Master discipleship class is available to all who want to attend in the millennial reign and kingdom of our Lord. Until the time we can physically sit at His feet, we must do the next best thing, as Timothy did, and come back to the foundation of the scriptures and learn the Torah foundation that can make us strong with the wisdom of the Word. Notice that training in righteousness is not the same as the imputed righteousness given as credit and a gift at salvation. The Torah Word will help you grow in that righteousness by teaching and training on how to walk that righteousness out. I call that practical righteousness. Most people today have learned about positional righteousness but not the practical. The Master Discipleship maker Yeshua trained his disciples in both. To forsake all is not popular. This new generation is dying for things of no lasting or eternal value because they have not been challenged to give and forsake all in the way of Yeshua and Abraham. Truthfully, it is uncomfortable for me to even write about this and I hope you will not be offended if I ask you, are you willing to forsake all to follow Yeshua?

Luke 9:62 TLV But Yeshua said to him, "No one who has put his hand to the plow and looked back is fit for the kingdom of God."

Chapter Three: Discipleship in the Book of Acts

As we begin to look at what was happening in the book of Acts, we must ask the Lord to help us not allow the opaque and obscured understandings of religion to continue to mislead the future of the congregation of the Lord as it has been for so many generations. I grew up as a Jewish boy and "got saved" at fifteen and was blessed to become involved in an amazing church and family. However, back then, we knew nothing about walking according to the Torah nor did we know much about

Messianic Judaism other than their practice of "traditions". The church we were accustomed to loved God's Word and believed it from cover to cover. The book of Acts was a goal, something to study and aspire to. They turned the world upside down. They were doing signs, wonders, and miracles. Making disciples was happening and we wanted it all too! We just didn't know, at the time, that the way of the book of Acts was founded on the Torah. Sometimes translations in the Bible are slanted against the Torah. Not having the correct context of the people and time of the writings, a misunderstanding can naturally occur. One such misunderstanding has occurred concerning the Gentiles or nations that were coming into the Kingdom in the book of Acts. This has become a divisive issue that has kept "New Testament Christians" separated from those who believe in Yeshua-Jesus and believe that the Torah is not only valid but a way of life for everyone who comes to faith. The naturally born Jews, in the book of Acts, are zealous for the Torah as the scripture says, and they are also believers in the power of the resurrection and put their faith in Yeshua as Lord. The gentile, or "former gentiles", as I like to say, are not told to forsake the law as most people think. In fact, it is the very opposite of that. The book of Acts is not only a continuation of the gospels but a renewal of the power and fire given with the Torah on Mount Sinai to the "first fruit" believers in Yeshua, the promised prophet who would come like Moses and teach the people obedience. Once again, God gave the nations that gathered at the Temple for Shavuot or Pentecost the opportunity to repeat what Israel said at Sinai. "We will do and we will hear"! As these "born again nations" are coming into the faith and covenant with Yeshus-Jesus and receiving the witness and confirmation of the Holy Spirit with evidence of tongues and prophecy, no one can deny that something is happening regarding restoration. Listen to the words of the Apostle Peter.

Acts 3:18-23 TLV18 But what God foretold through the mouth of all His prophets—that His Messiah was to suffer—so He has fulfilled. 19 Repent, therefore, and return—so your sins might be blotted out, 20 so times of relief might come from the presence of Adonai and He might send Yeshua, the Messiah appointed for you. 21 Heaven must receive Him, until the time of the restoration of all the things that God spoke about long ago through the mouth of His holy prophets. 22 Moses said, 'Adonai your God will raise up for you a Prophet like me from among your brothers. Hear and obey Him in all that He shall say to you. 23 And it shall be that every soul that will not listen to that Prophet shall be completely cut off from the people.'

As Jews and non-Jews come to faith in Yeshua, the congregation of the Lord begins to grow and with that rapid growth some issues that were already prevalent in the time of the gospels and beyond begin to influence and affect the congregation. When diversity of opinions in doctrine is not dealt with, it can cause division and disunity in the people. When the Spirit of God begins to move, one of the works of the Spirit will expose and bring to the surface issues that need to be uncovered so the truth can be taught. The Holy Spirit and the Word are one. God is seeking worshippers who are both Spirit-led and full of the Word of Truth. You cannot have one and be in balance. We need two wings to fly a plane and that is the same with the walk and way of Messiah. It is both Spirit and Truth.

In chapter fifteen of the Book of Acts, you will find four starting places given by the Apostles to the ones coming into faith and obedience from the nations. When someone comes to the Lord from a background of idolatry or worldliness, they come as "babes in Messiah". All their lives they have lived a certain way. They were taught that way as the normal way of that culture or belief system. So deep in the soul (appetites, desires, emotions, and intellect) these strongholds of the mind and body have been the way for the nations coming to Messiah. In the Bible, the stranger was a "ger" who would dwell among or with Israel to learn about their God. The stranger would be taught the same decrees, judgments, and Torah that the Israelites would learn. An age-old controversy going back to Jacob and the Shechemites was, "When do you circumcise a convert?" In

Shechem, Jacob's sons told the nation to get circumcised first to prove the worthiness of the covenant. This did not end well, because the covenant of circumcision was something they did not know nor understand. The Shechemites wanted the blessings of the relationship but did not understand the cost of that blessing as obedience to the God of Israel's instructions.

Numbers 15:15-16CJB 15 "The community will have the same rule for you as well as for the resident outsider. It will be a lasting statute throughout your generations. As for you, so for the outsider will it be before Adonai. 16 The same Torah and the same regulations will apply to both you and the outsider residing among you."

The standard for the stranger from the nations who wanted to be joined to Israel was to be the same as the native-born Israelite. The only problem then, in the book of Acts, was when these strangers were physically circumcised. Because of the many converts coming from the nations to believe in Yeshua and the God of Abraham, Isaac, and Jacob, this controversy reached a climax when some Pharisees wanted to force these new converts to be immediately circumcised after accepting Yeshua. Remember, the "ger" of the nations joining Israel was something that was looked upon by native Israelites as one to be treated with high esteem. Even today when someone converts to Judaism that person is heralded and not treated in any way as a second-class citizen. The reason for this is the same reason adopted children feel so special. They were chosen specifically by their parents. When a person accepts Yeshua-Jesus they, too, are adopted and chosen into the household of faith and the kingdom family.

If we go back and look at Abraham's "conversion" from idolatry into a covenant relationship with God, we will see a pattern and principle that was relevant in the book of Acts and for today. Abraham was seventy-five years old at the time of the encounter with El Shaddai, the living God. Notice, at the beginning of that relationship and for the next twenty-four years, Abraham was not circumcised until he had walked with God for many years, learning and growing in his faith.

Genesis 17:23-24 TLV 23 Then Abraham took Ishmael his son and all of his house-born slaves and all his purchased slaves—every male among the men of Abraham's house—and he circumcised the flesh of their foreskin on this very same day, just as God had spoken with him. 24 Abraham was 99 years old when he was circumcised in the flesh of his foreskin,

When Israel was redeemed from Egypt and started on the journey in the wilderness that took forty years, we learn that during those forty years, the commanded circumcision of the boys at eight days old was not being done. The Israelites, in the desert, had received the Torah and the commandments, but because they were still in process, they would not complete the circumcision until they were ready to cross into the land at Gilgal.

Joshua 5:4-5 TLV 4 Now this is the reason why Joshua circumcised: all the people that came out of Egypt who were males—all the men of war—had died in the wilderness along the way after they came out of Egypt. 5 Though all the people that came out were circumcised, none of the people who were born in the wilderness along the way as they came out of Egypt had been circumcised.

The point of this understanding is to help you understand the controversy that was still very strong as new believers from the nations were being added to the faith, which could not be denied. Yet, these brand new converts were not physically circumcised, but rather, they had a spiritual circumcision not made with the hands of man, but the word of God. Now after this what would be the protocol of the congregation?

Acts 15:1-5 AMP Some men came down from Judea and began teaching the brothers, "Unless you are circumcised in accordance with the custom of Moses, you cannot be saved." 2 Paul and Barnabas disagreed greatly and debated with them, so it was determined that Paul and Barnabas and some of the others from their group would go up to Jerusalem to the apostles and the elders [and confer with them] concerning this issue. 3 So, after being supplied and sent on their way by the church, they went through both Phoenicia and Samaria telling in detail the conversion of the Gentiles, and they brought great joy to all the believers. 4 When they arrived in Jerusalem, they were received warmly by the church and the apostles and the elders, and they reported to them all the things that God had accomplished through them. 5 But some from the sect of the Pharisees who had believed in Jesus as the Messiah] stood up and said, "It is necessary to circumcise the Gentile converts and to direct them to observe the Law of Moses."

Something good was happening. Coverts to Yeshua were being made and the report would testify the Holy Spirit had been poured out on the Gentile converts and no one could stop it. God had ordained the nations to come to faith in Yeshua even by the Apostle Peter's mouth. What was in question by a Pharisee, was that to be saved, you must command them to get circumcised and keep Torah. The problem with this statement is that being circumcised and keeping Torah is an outgrowth of salvation and not how salvation is accomplished. Salvation is and always was, by faith, and then corresponding actions that demonstrate faith and trust in Adonai. Keep in mind that this controversy was not about circumcision on the eighth day as required by Torah, but rather circumcision as a mark in a man's flesh revealing his covenant with the God of Israel.

Acts chapter fifteen was and still is a misunderstood portion of scripture. Many "Christians" will cite this as proof that you don't need to obey Torah or physical circumcision. But, is that really being taught here? I humbly submit to you that Acts chapter fifteen is the key chapter in the book of Acts as to the success of the great fruit. The Torah would be learned by all the new converts regardless if they were natural-born citizens or from the nations as you will see in just a moment. The Apostles were so wise in remembering the story of Shechem of how Simeon and Levi forced circumcision after the rape of Dinah. Now Simon Peter reverses the mistakes of the past and gives the new, former gentile converts, a starting place in their faith that helps them to immediately grow in grace and also fellowship with the naturally born Jewish converts who were also Zealous for the Torah and faith in Yeshua as the way to salvation.

Acts 15:19-21 CSB19 Therefore, in my judgment, we should not cause difficulties for those among the Gentiles who turn to God, 20 but instead we should write to them to abstain from things polluted by idols, from sexual immorality, from eating anything that has been strangled, and from blood. 21 For since ancient times, Moses has had those who proclaim him in every city, and every Sabbath day he is read aloud in the synagogues."

The leaders of the congregation of the Lord gave four starting points for the nations coming into faith and from that point they can join the congregation on Shabbat and learn the Torah of Moses which has been done since ancient times. As we move into the next chapter let us now dig into these four starting points and the Torah Way that followed.

Chapter Four: The Secret Sauce

My wife Lisa and I love this statement from one of our associates who told us, while talking about the Lord and His blessing, that "we have the secret sauce". These associates had grown up in the "traditional" way and had learned just like us. When my wife and I were awakened to begin to practice the roots of our faith, our lives were radically transformed as well as an entire congregation who joined us on our journey, very slowly, by learning, or should I say re-learning our identity as connected to Abraham and Israel and what it truly means to be grafted in. I want to emphasize that we told the people from the beginning, that it's a starting point and it seemed to resonate with our believers from the nations. It only made sense to name our congregation "Save the Nations". I told them that they don't have to do all these things, but they get to! We said it so much, that everyone knows the saying. Of course, that was the starting point. Now, our new statement is "I get to, then I want to, then I love to and then no one can stop me because I can't live without it"! A starting point is a way to begin to walk, but it is not the full picture that will continue to evolve as you begin and move from the different stages of growth: an infant to a child, to a youth, and then to a mature adult. All of this takes time and actually, is one of the ways I like to look at discipleship. It takes time to be discipled.

So what is the secret sauce? It is a very simple recipe and the key to that sauce is doing and guarding Shabbat, the Appointed Times, the Moedim, and studying, learning, and applying the weekly Torah portions. When you do these simple things, get ready for exponential and supernatural growth in your walk with the Lord. As you walk this walk, you will experience so many blessings that it will be impossible to count them! I know you might be thinking the Torah portions are for the Jews right? I will never forget my first Hebrew Roots conference with Dr. Holissa Alewine, who now is like a spiritual mom to my wife and me and the very best teacher and model of the Torah. I know, I had a class on 144,000 reasons to do the Torah portions. Guess what? I would not and even refused to go to her class! I was thinking to myself, "I can't do the Torah portions and I certainly can't bring them to our congregation. Everyone will say, even more, that I am trying to make everyone Jewish!" I can't tell you how wrong I was. It was not until years later, after beginning to study the Torah portions and experiencing exponential and supernatural growth, that I introduced them to my wife and she began to mature and grow too. Every week she would say. This Torah portion "kicked my ...." We would laugh because it was so true. Somehow every Torah portion was right on time and most of the time you would see what you are studying in the world and especially in the land of Israel.

Let's go back to the book of Acts as the prototype and model of discipleship in the congregation with nations being joined to Israel and now in their midst just like the "geo-stranger" who dwelled with them.

Acts 15:19-21 The Voice (VOICE) 19 So here is my counsel: we should not burden these outsiders who are turning to God. 20 We should instead write a letter, instructing them to abstain from four things: first, things associated with idol worship; second, sexual immorality; third, food killed by strangling; and fourth, blood. 21 My reason for these four exceptions is that in every city there are Jewish communities where, <u>for generations</u>, <u>the laws of Moses have been proclaimed;</u> and on every Sabbath, Moses is read in synagogues everywhere.

ACTS 15 TLV VS: 21 For Moses from ancient generations has had in every city those who proclaim him, since he is read in all the synagogues every Shabbat."

In Acts Chapter 15 they started the new believers from the nations with four "keys" which were commandments from "Exodus & Leviticus ". Then they were to learn Moses (Torah) every Sabbath.

*Leviticus 17:12-16, Exodus 22:31, Exodus 34:15-17, Leviticus

3:17 ,Leviticus 17:8-13, Leviticus 18: 6-27 (References to study)

Look again at the four starting points after receiving Yeshua so they can be in union with mostly native Jewish believers. Notice these Torah instructions are not the end but the beginning and a foundation for walking with Yeshua and in His Kingdom Ways.

I summarized the 4 things to make them simple and memorable:

1. Idolatry
2. Immorality
3. Cruelty
4. Purity

<u>Strangled</u> - According to Harper's Bible commentary things strangled

meant not "rabbinically slaughtered." Since the only things rabbinically slaughtered were clean animals, this is clear evidence the grafted in, former gentile believers, were taught from the beginning to eat only clean animals. They understood that eating unclean was part of the idolatry of the nations that would be an open door, keeping them tied to the Babylonian and Egyptian system of mixture and confusion, the way of sin and death.

The word for strangled also means to choke like you are denying breath to the animal. This has the same root word in the parable of the sower that talks about the weeds "choking" the new life out of the new growth. In the parable, when you study it, it will bring you to the "other" nations that Israel would or could not dispossess which became thorns in their sides and pricks in their eyes. The nation's ways have been a stumbling block for Israel and for God's people today in the same way. These four starting points are to get the new believer a strong foundation that will not choke the word they received from being fruitful.

Mark 4:19 KJV And the cares of this world, and the deceitfulness of riches, and the lusts of other things entering in, choke the word, and it becometh unfruitful.

The question of when a convert gets circumcised has been a long-standing controversy and many of the New Testament teachings were because of the "war" between the two Rabbinic schools of Hillel and Shammai. Circumcision was a sign of covenant for males to be done on the 8th day of birth. According to the House of Shammai, a new convert must immediately be circumcised to show his obedience to the covenant of Abraham. The House of Hillel took a different view that allowed for the convert to first show himself to understand the Torah and eventually circumcision, but not be the first thing.

- Abram entered into covenant at seventy-five years of age but was not circumcised until he was 99 years old, 24 years later. (Genesis 15,17)

- The children of Israel, for 40 years, did not circumcise their sons in the wilderness. (Joshua 5:5-7)

In both cases, the physical circumcision did not precede the spiritual circumcision which the Apostles conferred to be the correct way. Eventually, the physical followed the spiritual. Circumcision in the Hebrew understanding, is cutting away the physical barrier to being sensitive to the Torah and the way of Adonai. It is a prophecy that all those connected to Israel will be spiritually sensitive to Messiah to come.

As a reminder, we know that the Shechemites, who did get circumcised "first", were not willing to sincerely follow the Torah, but only entered into covenant to get Jacob's daughter and wealth. (Genesis 34:20-24)

Circumcision should begin in the heart and never be forced on those from the nations as something you must do immediately, but rather after they learn and grow in the commandments and Torah. Then they will realize that they "get to and want to" because it pleases the Lord when we "Shema" and hear and obey His commandments.

Romans 2:29 AMP29 But he is a Jew who is one inwardly; and [true] circumcision is circumcision of the heart, by the Spirit, not by [the fulfillment of] the letter [of the Law]. His praise is not from men but from God.

I don't want to spend a lot of time on these 4 things, but I want you to see the former gentile believers were given Torah and specifically Laws from Leviticus or Vayikra, which means to call and also, the book of Exodus or Shemot meaning "names". Hidden in these laws is the truth of a calling to purity and identity that is separate from the world.

Please remember the four starting points were taken right out of Torah being decrees for both the native Israelites and the converts who were coming into faith in the God of the patriarchs. The Apostle Paul in the book of Corinthians will build on the foundation of the book of Acts. Also, remember God chose him who was a master of the Torah and the Hebrew Bible to train those coming in from the Nations the ways of Adonai.

2 Corinthians 6:14-18 TLV Preserving Sanctity in God's Living Temple 14 Do not be unequally yoked with

unbelievers.[c] For what partnership is there between righteousness and lawlessness? Or what fellowship does light have with darkness? 15 What harmony does Messiah have with Belial[d]? Or what part does a believer have in common with an unbeliever? 16 What agreement does God's Temple have with idols?[e] For we are the temple of the living God —just as God said, "I will dwell in them and walk among them; and I will be their God, and they shall be My people.[f] 17 Therefore, come out from among them, and be separate, says Adonai. Touch no unclean thing. [g] Then I will take you in.[h] 18 I will be a father to you, and you shall be My sons and daughters, says Adonai-Tzva'ot."[I] Footnotes

- [2 Corinthians 6:2](#) Isa. 49:8; cf. Isa.

55:6.

- 2 Corinthians 6:10 cf. Ps. 118:18.
- 2 Corinthians 6:14 cf. Deut. 22:9-11.
- 2 Corinthians 6:15 A spelling variant here of Grk. belial, the devil; Heb. b'liya'al, worthlessness, possibly a wordplay on Heb. b'li 'ol, without a yoke.
- 2 Corinthians 6:16 cf. Ezek. 8:3, 10.
- 2 Corinthians 6:16 cf. Exod. 29:45; Lev. 26:11-12; Jer. 32:38; Ezek. 37:27.
- 2 Corinthians 6:17 cf. Isa. 52:11.
- 2 Corinthians 6:17 cf. Ezek. 20:34, 41.
- 2 Corinthians 6:18 Grk. Kurios Pantokrator (Lord Almighty); cf. 2 Sam. 7:8, 14(2 Ki. 7:8, 14 LXX); 1 Chr. 17:13; Isa. 43:6; Hos. 12:6(5).

I left you the references here so you can study in the future at your own pace the richness of the confirmation over and over by the Apostles.

The foundation of discipleship starts with faith and trust in the God who brought you out of Egypt and transferred you from darkness to light and death to life. The same journey began for Israel by putting the blood of the lamb on their homes. They went through that bloody door into a new beginning being baptized in the Red Sea and into Moses; a metaphor for Torah.

Exodus 20:1-2 TLV Then God spoke all these words saying, 2 "I am Adonai your God, who brought you out of the land of Egypt, out of the house of bondage. 3 "You shall have no other gods before Me.

The first step for anyone coming to Adonai-Elohim is recognizing Him as your redeemer and deliverer from the bondage of Egypt. Then he demands for all not to have any other god in His presence. This is the starting point the Apostles gave as a model to grow up the new believers in the book of Acts.

1. Idol Worship
2. Sexual Immorality

A companion to idol worship would be sexual immorality. Both are acts of unfaithfulness and you really can't separate them. Idolatry is Adultery and Adultery is Idolatry. They both are bringing another into a sacred relationship.

Acts 15:20 But that we write unto them, that they abstain from <u>pollutions</u> **G234** of idols, and from fornication, and from things strangled, and from blood.

G234ἀλίσγεμα alísgema, al-is'-ghem-ah; from ἀλισγέω alisgéō (to soil); (ceremonially) defilement:— pollution.

The Hebrew equivalent of this word is:

H1351 גָּאַל gâ'al, gaw-al'; a primitive root, (rather identified with H1350, through the idea of freeing, i.e. repudiating); to soil or (figuratively) desecrate:—defile, pollute, stain.

Daniel 1:8 But Daniel purposed in his heart that he would not defile H1351 himself with the portion of the king's meat, nor with the wine which he drank: therefore he requested of the prince of the eunuchs that he might not defile H1351 himself.

There seems to be a strong connection in the Bible with what someone eats and consumes with a defiling or soiling of man's body as a temple in connection to the altar known as the "table of the Lord".

Gesenius' Hebrew-Chaldee Lexicon

II. גָּאַל a word of the later [?] Hebrew, not used in Kal, *to be polluted, impure*, i. q. Chald. גְּעַל; Ithpe. אִתְגְּעַל to be polluted.

PIEL גֵּאַל *to pollute, to defile*, Mal. 1:7.

PUAL.—(1) *to be polluted*; part. מְגֹאָל *polluted, impure, unclean*, of food, Mal. 1:7, 12.

(2) *declared impure*, i.e. *to be removed*, as a priest from sacred ministry, Ezr. 2:62; Neh. 7:64; compare Syriac ܓܥܠ *to cast away, reject*, and גָּעַל Hiphil.

NIPHAL נְגֹאָל Zeph. 3:1, and נִגְאַל Isa. 59:3; Lam. 4:14 (which form is like the passive Conj. VII. in Arabic انقبل), *polluted, defiled, stained.*

HIPHIL, *to pollute, to stain*, as a garment with blood, Isa. 63:3. The form אֶגְאַלְתִּי for הִגְאַלְתִּי imitates the Syriac.

HITHPAEL, *to pollute oneself*, with unclean food, Dan. 1:8. Hence—

Malachi 1:7 Ye offer polluted H1351 bread upon mine altar; and ye say, Wherein have we polluted H1351 thee? In that ye say, The table of the

LORD is contemptible.

Acts 15:18-21 BLT   18 "All of God's works are known to him from eternity. 19 Therefore my judgment is that we don't trouble those from among the Gentiles who turn to God, 20 but that we write to them that they abstain from the pollution of idols, from sexual immorality, from what is <u>strangled,</u> and <u>from blood</u>. 21 For Moses from generations of old has in every city those who preach him, being read in the synagogues every Sabbath."

The four prohibitions were given as a starting point and the last two deal specifically with eating blood and how an animal would be ritually slaughtered. If you put yourself back in the time from when this was written, it would be readily understood that all these coming from the nations, to join the Kedoship-Saints and Holy ones of the Lord's congregation, would not be able to keep eating unclean foods of their culture nor could they go to the market and buy food that had been previously offered to idols. From this foundation, these new disciples who were grafted in and adopted would begin to learn the Godly traditions that had sustained those believing Jews for thousands of years. This starting point was necessary to keep the unity of the faith and not to pollute the people and land of the people of Israel. The book of Acts is the prototype and has the secret sauce embedded already as a model for us today to follow. What day was the gathering for God's people? Shabbat, the 7th day. Did they keep the Feasts? Yes! Did the people gather at the synagogue? Yes! Did they still bring sacrifices and first fruits to Jerusalem and the Temple? Yes!

The role of making disciples (pupils, learners) is the very last thing Yeshua taught before his ascension. The importance of discipling all nations is as a command for all believers to follow.

Matthew 28:19-20 The Passion Translation (TPT) 19 Now go in my authority and make disciples of all nations, baptizing them in the name of the Father, the Son, and the Holy Spirit. 20 And teach them to faithfully follow[all that I have commanded you. And never forget that I am with you every day, even to the completion of this age."

We must realize the commands of Yeshua were the same as Torah. He was and is the Torah-Word made flesh. If someone is born Jewish or with an understanding of the Torah, the starting place will not be the same as the person who is steeped in the ways and traditions of the nations. For when that person comes to faith in Yeshua and receives the Holy Spirit, they begin a journey learning how to walk out that new faith in Spirit and Truth. At first, they do not know about God's ways, His days, and what pleases God. Over time this person will have a transformation. (Romans 12:1-2)

The Secret Sauce:

1. Keep and Guard Shabbat
2. Celebrate God's Moedim
3. Study to do the Torah

That simple recipe will begin to align you for your divine assignment. As you follow what our Lord has given for your good, your spiritual eyes will not be clouded by the nations. You will have the discernment so you won't be trapped in the enemy's plans or web of deceit. These simple things will help you to be in Divine Alignment for your Divine Assignment.

- At the Right Place
- At the Right Time
- With the Right People
- Doing the Right Things

DIVINE ALIGNMENT FOR YOUR DIVINE ASSIGNMENT

- AT THE RIGHT PLACE
- AT THE RIGHT TIME
- WITH THE RIGHT PEOPLE
- DOING THE RIGHT THINGS

SUPERNATURAL DISCIPLESHIP

THE SECRET SAUCE

- **KEEP AND GUARD SHABBAT**
- **CELEBRATE GOD'S MOEDIM**
- **STUDY TO DO TORAH**

SUPERNATURAL DISCIPLESHIP

Chapter Five: The Torah Portions

So please remember I never wanted to do the Torah portions called the "Parashah" in Hebrew. I was so afraid I would push my congregation over the edge and they would tell me I had gone too far. So back in 2020, in the summertime, I began a Zoom teaching to gather my people for a time to learn the Word. I would usually teach whatever was on my heart. I had been learning and studying Torah, but I was not even thinking about it for my people until a leader asked me to teach her what I was learning. I told her I would send her to my friend in Tennessee who was a good teacher and knew way more than I did. After a few weeks, I was convicted as the Lord asked me why I was sending my sheep to another shepherd to learn the Torah. One Wednesday, shortly after that, I decided I would teach the Torah portion, but not tell the people what I was doing. The people responded and loved the teaching so the next week I did the same thing. After two weeks I told the people I was teaching them Torah and began to send them the Torah portions to study and read all week long. At that time I did not know how these Torah portions even worked. On a trip to Israel, I learned that the Torah portion for that week ended with Shabbat, and the people, during the time of Yeshua-Jesus, would study the portion from the first day of the week until the 7th day. I never knew that and you might not either.

So, now on Saturday night after Shabbat, I send my people the Torah portions to read and study during the week. In that Torah portion, there will be a certain prescribed text from the five books of Moses as well as a Haf-Torah, which is a portion usually from the Prophets. I also send the prescribed portion from the Psalms for each portion as well as a New Testament reading.

You might be thinking like I did, that the Torah Portions are only a Jewish thing. But remember, Acts 15 tells us that after the four foundational prohibitions, every week Moses or Torah is being taught and read from ancient times. This is where we get the Torah portion understanding. All the disciples learned the same Torah because over and over in the Torah we know the stranger must learn the same Torah as the native. Those who teach the false "Noahide" laws, which aren't even in the Bible, do not want anyone but native-born Israelites to do what God has commanded for all men. It is just another way to separate instead of unify God's people.

Acts 15:21 TLV For Moses from ancient generations has had in every city those who proclaim him, since he is read in all the synagogues every Shabbat."

What worked, in such a powerful way in the book of Acts and the early congregations, has now been replaced with inspirational and topical messages and a system of discipleship and ministry geared to certain subjects or affinity or age groups. All of that makes sense because people like to gather around what draws or connects to them. Now if you are doing ministry like that, do not feel condemned because that is what is common in our culture. The Torah way of supernatural discipleship and growth is not a need-based or affinity type of system or model. Once you start and make the commitment, please don't deviate from the Torah cycle and portions. Stay with it and don't worry where or when you begin, just start now! This supernatural system of discipleship, in the course of a year, will deal with and teach everything you or a congregation and family will go through. It is like God designed a master manual for His people and when you study and do the manual it will cover everything that pertains to life and godliness. If you do this for yourself, or if you are a leader, then you will discover the wisdom of the Torah. It will do all the heavy lifting and you won't have to go around wondering if people are being discipled, because the Torah will disciple the people. The Torah will deal with finances, marriage and relationships, family issues, sexual and gender issues and those who study the Torah will absolutely know what the Way of the Messiah is. If you have never done the Torah portions, please begin and hold yourself accountable. Don't be distracted by the popular itch ear stuff. Stay focused.

Find a good Torah teacher and learn from him. If your Rabbi or Pastor teaches Torah, then sit faithfully and glean the bounty and feast on that Word of life.

Luke 4:16- 21 TLV 16 And He came to Natzeret, where He had been raised. As was His custom, He went into the synagogue on Shabbat, and He got up to read. 17 When the scroll of the prophet Isaiah was handed to Him, He unrolled the scroll and found the place where it was written, 18 "The Ruach Adonai is on me, because He has anointed me to proclaim Good News to the poor. He has sent me to proclaim release to the captives and recovery of sight to the blind, to set free the oppressed, 19 and to proclaim the year of Adonai's favor." 20 He closed the scroll, gave it back to the attendant, and sat down. All eyes in the synagogue were focused on Him. 21 Then He began to tell them, "Today this Scripture has been fulfilled in your ears."

Notice Yeshua was handed the scroll of Isaiah. He read from the prophet portion of that week. The leader in the Synagogue was responsible for the Torah readings and our Lord not only upheld but affirmed that protocol of the Torah cycle.

It is believed that after the Temple's destruction by the Babylonians in 583 BC, the Torah portions were begun in the days of Nehemiah and Ezra as they began to repair and rebuild the Temple. The tradition probably goes back further and was passed down orally over time. We know the book of Acts says that from ancient times Torah was taught, we just don't know how long ago that really was. During the time of Yeshua and the book of Acts, we do know these Torah portions were established and followed. These Torah portions are also one of the greatest ways for all of God's people to be unified as we are all studying and learning to do the same thing at the same time. Now that is Divine Alignment!

[1]Parashat appears in manuscripts as early as the Dead Sea Scrolls, in which the division is generally similar to that found in the Masoretic text. [6] The idea of spacing between portions, including the idea of "open" and "closed" portions, is mentioned in

early midrashic literature[7] and the Talmud. Early Masoretic lists detailing the Babylonian tradition include a systematic and detailed discussion of exactly where portions begin and which type they are.

1 Corinthians 11:2 Now I praise you, brethren, that ye remember me in all things, and keep the ordinances, G3862 as I delivered them to you.

2 Thessalonians 2:15 Therefore, brethren, stand fast, and hold the traditions G3862 which ye have been taught, whether by word, or our epistle.

2 Thessalonians 3:6 Now we command you, brethren, in the name of our Lord Jesus Christ, that

ye withdraw yourselves from every brother that walketh disorderly, and not after the tradition G3862 which he received of us.

G3862 parádosis, par-ad'-os-is; from G3860; transmission, i.e. (concretely) a precept; specially, the Jewish traditionary law:—ordinance, tradition.

When the Apostle Paul, the Master student and teacher of Torah, wrote to the disciples, he reminded them to uphold and keep the traditions that he taught. Although the specifics are not known, he is adamant about believers keeping godly traditions, such as lighting candles on Shabbat, blessing one another with your words, and eating and blessing the Cup and

Challah. All are ways to affirm the faith of Yeshua and do the commandments as an act of love. There should be no doubt in your mind that the early congregations in the book of Acts were learning and doing the Torah portions.

2 Timothy 3:14-16 TLV14 You, however, continue in what you have learned and what you have become convinced of. For you know from whom you have learned, 15 and that from childhood you have known the sacred writings that are able to make you wise, leading to salvation through trusting in Messiah Yeshua. 16 All Scripture is inspired by God and useful for teaching, for reproof, for restoration, and for training in righteousness,

The scriptures of that time were not those we read today in the New Testament. The foundation of scripture was what had been taught from the time of Moses until the present day. The scriptures of the New Testament will confirm everything in the Tanakh, the Hebrew Bible. The Apostle Paul's letters will become part of the New Testament Canon.

2 Peter 3:15-16 CJB15 And think of our Lord's patience as deliverance, just as our dear brother Sha'ul also wrote you, following the wisdom God gave him. 16 Indeed, he speaks about these things in all his letters. They contain some things that are hard to understand, things which the uninstructed and unstable distort, to

their own destruction, as they do the other Scriptures.

Even during Peter's day, Paul's letters were misunderstood. During the millennial reign, our Lord Himself will expound these teachings and show all His beloved sheep the true understanding of what Paul meant. For now, the more you study the Torah portions you will see the New Testament, the Brit Hadashah, with new eyes and revelation that has been hidden. Last-day knowledge and revelation are now exploding among those who are studying Torah. I believe something very big is on the horizon and all the earth will be filled with the Knowledge of the Lord as the waters cover the sea. The nations are being awakened to their inheritance connected to Father Abraham through Yeshua the Messiah. These are special times to be alive on the earth. We like to tell people, when you pray for revival, pray also that the revival would be sustained and not lost or diminished. To my knowledge, since the time of the book of Acts, we have not had a sustained revival because the wineskin of the Supernatural discipleship in the Torah has not been done. Imagine and dream of revival, outpouring and great awakening to come to the nations with the Torah.

Revelation 14:12 TLV   Here is the perseverance of the kedoshim—those who keep the commandments of God and the faith of Yeshua.

Chapter Six: Do you see what I see?

The process of discipleship takes time. Even with your own children, who are raised and trained in your home with your values, your example, and love, the process takes time. Because of that time-tested bond, they know instinctively and without a second guess what is desired and expected because they have caught the spirit of the house. When Yeshua trained His disciples, in that three-year process of being in very close proximity with Rabbi Yeshua and hearing and seeing, day after day, the things no one else was privileged to see, and learning at His feet, they were catching the heart of the Lord by His actions and words and by things he didn't do or need to say. This is what happens when you are around someone long enough, especially if there is intention and purpose of discipleship.

Luke 6:40 TLV A disciple is not above his teacher, but everyone who is fully trained will be like his teacher.

Matthew 10:25 CJB It is enough for a talmid that he become like his rabbi, and a slave like his master. Now if people have called the head of the house Ba'al-Zibbul, how much more will they malign the members of his household!

At the end of the process, the disciple will be like the one who trained him. Yeshua is letting His beloved disciples know that they are family and the apprenticeship is for the spiritual children to become mature adults, fully equipped, and trained to do the same for the next generation to come. Yeshua had to be a disciple of His cousin John and also of Moses. Yeshua often quoted Torah, including the book of Deuteronomy, and His favorite, the Psalms. We know Moses prophesied of a prophet who would come with his same spirit. The prophet like Him is Yeshua. For remember, the disciple shall be as His teacher.

Acts 3:33-26 TLV 22 Moses said, 'Adonai your God will raise up for you a Prophet like me from among your brothers. Hear and obey Him in all that

He shall say to you. 23 And it shall be that every soul that will not listen to that Prophet shall be completely cut off from the people. '[c] 24 Indeed, all the prophets who have spoken from Samuel on have announced these days. 25 You are the sons of the prophets and also of the covenant that God cut with your fathers,[d] saying to Abraham, 'In your seed shall all the families of the earth be blessed. '[e] 26 God raised up His Servant and sent Him first to you, to bless you all by turning each of you from your wicked ways."

Footnotes

C.   Acts   3:24   cf.   Deut.

18:15-19(LXX); Lev. 23:29(LXX).

D. Acts 3:25 cf. Exod. 24:8; Heb. 10:16.

E. Acts 3:26 cf. Gen. 12:3; 22:18.

A great lesson is in the story of the Samaritans who did not receive Yeshua because they disliked that He was going to Jerusalem. The disciples asked to call fire down from heaven but Yeshua said "You do not know what manner of spirit you are of!" That is so interesting because Elijah did call down fire more than once, but his disciple Elisha, who had a double portion of that spirit, never called down fire from heaven, not even once.

I believe the reason is hidden in this scripture.

2 Kings 1:14 KJV 14 Look, fire has come down from heaven and burned up the first two captains of fifties with their fifties. But let my life now be precious in your sight."

The spirit of Elijah was not just one of fiery judgment, but also of mercy for those who did not know any better. The Samaritans were confused as to where, what, and who to worship. But Yeshua was trying to teach His disciples to catch the right spirit, not one of death, but of life. He wanted them to know the last part of the scripture when the leader asked for his life to be precious and valuable to Elijah. We must see all people with that kind of potential, to save them instead of destroying them whenever possible.

Luke 9:55-56 WEB55 But he turned and rebuked them, "You don't know of what kind of spirit you are. 56 For the Son of Man didn't come to destroy men's lives, but to save them."

This is so important because I have been hearing reports of how some teachers and students of the Torah Way are angry at the traditional Christian church and are demeaning, and condemning them for not walking the way they are. Many of them are full of harshness, are carrying past hurts, and have become proud instead of humble. Many are like the disciples who wanted to call down fire because the Samaritans weren't doing it right. Today we hear things like "they aren't pronouncing the sacred name correctly" or "they are not saying God's real name and are too rabbinic". We can always find something someone isn't doing correctly like we think they should, but are we to call down the heavenly fire? Or, should we instead be kind, merciful, and forgiving and pray for them? All of this will continue to divide the Kingdom instead of unifying it.

Let's return to Elijah and Elisha, two of the most powerful prophets in the history of Israel. A key to understanding their ministry is the fact that, even though they were living in the time of the divided Kingdoms of Judah and the House of Israel, God allowed these great prophetic voices to be spokesmen in the House of Israel, which was steeped in the idolatry of Baal and Ashtoreth. If anyone was doing it wrong, it was those who were following Jeraboam's example of golden calf worship in Bethel and Dan. Creating His own counterfeit 8th month Moedim Appointed time. Yet in all this, God has Elijah traveling the land and ministering to the people.

2 Kings 2:1-7 TLV Now it came to pass, when Adonai was about to take up Elijah by a whirlwind into heaven, that Elijah went with Elisha from Gilgal. 2 Elijah said to Elisha, "Stay here please, for Adonai has sent me on to Bethel." But Elisha said, "As Adonai lives, and as you live, I will not leave you." So they went down to Bethel. 3 Then the sons of the prophets at Bethel came out to Elisha and said

to him, "Do you know that Adonai is going to take your master away from over you today?"

He said, "Yes, I know. Be silent." 4 Then Elijah said to him, "Elisha, stay here please, for Adonai has sent me on to Jericho." But he said, "As Adonai lives and as you live, I will not leave you." So they came to Jericho. 5 Then the sons of the prophets at Jericho approached Elisha and said to him, "Do you know that Adonai is going to take away your master from over you today?" He replied, "Yes, I know. Be silent."

6 Then Elijah said to him, "Stay here please, for Adonai has sent me to the Jordan."

But he said, "As Adonai lives and as you live, I will not leave you." So both of them went on. 7 Then 50 of the sons of the prophets went and stood aside at a distance from them, while the two of them stood by the Jordan.

Apparently, by the Spirit, all the sons of the prophets knew that it was time for Elijah's ministry to end and He was going to be taken by the Lord in some way that day. The sons of the prophets were a little different than Elisha. For many years he poured water or served Elijah faithfully and I believe had caught his true spirit of saving lives and ministry to all the people. Elisha was a business person who was plowing behind twenty-four ox. That tells me he was willing to plow some rough ground. People of the earth and dirt can be hard ground sometimes, but Elisha was already prepared even before the start of his service to Elijah. After He forsook all in true discipleship form, he spent years learning, growing, and helping with humility and faithfulness for the Divine moment of transfer that might not have happened. You see Elisha was told by Elijah, multiple times, to leave him but Elisha refused. When God has called you, flesh and blood should not deter you, no matter what, you have to stay the course for the sake of the calling. At the beginning of Elisha's call, he was told by Elijah that He did not call him because Elisha needed to know it was God who calls, not man. Man can confirm it by the Spirit, but ultimately the call always has to come from above.

Elijah will make one final circuit and who will be with him? Elisha, who refused to leave. I believe he would not leave because he already saw what Elijah saw. He was living the call before the title and before the mantle would fall, he already was operating with the same anointing and spirit.

The four places were probably the circuit of ministry Elijah would readily journey. He started at Gilgal, then Bethel, Jericho, and the Jordan River. When Elijah saw that Elisha wouldn't leave he said:

2 Kings 2:8-10 TLV 8 Elijah then took his mantle, wrapped it together, and struck the waters, and they were divided here and there, so that they two of them crossed over on dry ground. 9 Now as they were crossing

over, Elijah said to Elisha, "Ask what I will do for you before I am taken from you." So Elisha said, "Please, let a double portion of your spirit be upon me." 10 He replied, "You have asked a hard thing. Nevertheless, if you see me when I am taken from you, it will be so to you; but if not, it will not be so."

Right after this, Elijah was carried away in the chariot of Israel, by a whirlwind up into the clouds. His mantle then fell to the ground and Elisha picked it up. Why did Elijah say it was hard? I believe Elijah was giving a secret coded message to Elisha of the price he will continue to pay to walk in that high calling among very hard and stubborn people that challenge the calling and make it difficult to persevere. Also, notice, the 50 called sons of the prophets watched at a distance. They did not see what Elisha saw and did not get the mantle that only Elisha was close enough to pick up.

H7185 קָשָׁה **qâshâh,** kaw-shaw'; a primitive root; properly, to be dense, i.e. tough or severe (in various applications):—be cruel, be fiercer, make grievous, be ((ask a), be in, have, seem, would) hard(-en, (labour), -ly, thing), be sore, (be, make) stiff(-en, (-necked)).

If you look deeper into the Hebrew language, you will find another way of looking at Elijah's words; " if you see what I see when I am taken, then you will have the double or firstborn portion of the anointing".

When Elisha stayed with Elijah on the final journey, it was proof that he not only physically saw, but spiritually he had lifted his eyes to see and catch the mantle of "Father -Father". Abba-Abba the son saw what the father saw and now the rightful, double portion was Elisha's.

What did Elisha see at those 4 places?

- Gilgal- Renewal of the Covenant

- Bethel-The House of God, the first altar of Abraham, and Jacob's ladder

- Jericho- The first fruit city with fortified walls taken by Joshua's obedience

- Jordan- The crossing through of Israel into the Promised Land

Elisha was being reminded of covenant renewal, the longing for a united kingdom where the House of God is restored and the first fruits are given to the Lord as every stronghold and high wall will be brought down through obedience.

The double portion is still available today, but do we see what Yeshua sees? Until we see what He sees, we won't have the double portion. The Lord left us a promise to do the greater things through the Spirit. Let's believe one day we will because that is our legacy and inheritance to do more and greater for His glory!

John 14 LB:12-16 12-13 "In solemn truth I tell you, anyone believing in me shall do the same miracles I have done, and even greater ones, because I am going to be with the Father. You can ask him for anything, using my name, and I will do it, for this will bring praise to the Father because of what I, the Son, will do for you. 14 Yes, ask anything, using my name, and I will do it! 15-16 "If you love me, obey me; and I will ask the Father and he will give you another Comforter, and he will never leave you.

A Discipleship Prayer

Heavenly Father I pray for your son or daughter right now that you would give them the spirit of wisdom and revelation in the knowledge of Yeshua. May your eyes be enlightened to know the hope of His calling, the riches of the glory of His inheritance in you, and to know the exceeding greatness of His power to you who believe and trust Him. May the Lord continually lead and guide you by His Word and His Spirit into the truth that leads to supernatural growth, enlargement, and exponential expansion over you and all connected to you. May you fulfill His calling and destiny as you are aligned divinely for your Divine assignment. May God put you with the right people, in the right place, at the right time, and always practice the right things. May God remove any wall or stumbling block keeping you from that high calling. May any, and all, generational curses that try to linger, be absolved and removed at the root level. May you embrace the way of the Torah and put into practice the keeping and guarding of the Shabbat, God's Moedim, and Appointed days and learn to obey the Torah. May you prosper and be in health as your soul prospers and no weapon formed be able to prosper against you. May revelation and spiritual knowledge continue to increase through and in your son and daughter as they keep themselves unspotted and unsoiled by the systems of Babylonian confusion and mixture and the realm of sin and death of Egypt.

Aaronic Benediction

Numbers 6:22-27 TLV 22 Again Adonai spoke to Moses saying, 23 "Speak to Aaron and to his sons saying: Thus you are to bless Bnei-Yisrael, by saying to them: 24 'Adonai bless you and keep you! 25 Adonai make His face to shine on you and be gracious to you! 26 Adonai turn His face toward you and grant you shalom!' 27 In this way they are to place My Name over Bnei-Yisrael, and so I will bless them."

BOOKS BY KENNETH S. ALBIN

YOU ARE BORN FOR THE EXTRAORDINARY

UPSIDE OF DOWN (Spanish, Portuguese, Russian)

THE MYSTERY OF THE CROWN

HACKED: THE HEBREW CHRISTIAN(Spanish, Portuguese, Russian)

CHRISTIANS GET TO CELEBRATE PASSOVER TOO!

NO MORE LEAVEN

HIT THE MARK

HIDDEN BLESSINGS REVEALED

TABERNACLES IT'S A CELEBRATION & NOT JUST AN OPTION!

HANUKKAH AND PURIM ARE FOR CHRISTIANS TOO

THE BLESSINGS OF PENTECOST

THE HEBREW CHRISTIAN LIFE

THE BLESSING OF ABRAHAM (Spanish, Portuguese)

Contact Information: for Ken Albin
www.savethenations.com /
www.hitthemarktorah.tv
info@savethenations.com

Kenny Albin, called by his Jewish mother, always believed he would be a "Rabbi". For over 30 years, as a born-again Jewish Christian pastor, Kenneth was awakened to walk in the way of His Messiah. He now teaches this Torah Way to all through Save the Nations based presently in South Florida but has influenced Israel, Brazil, and Nations around the world.

---

[1] https://en.wikipedia.org/wiki/Parashah